Read Well™

How Does Your
Garden Grow?

08 07 06 05 04 03   6 5 4 3 2 1

Edited by Lisa Howard and Sandra L. Knauke
Design and layout by Katherine Getta
Cover design by Sue Campbell
Production assistance by Karen Clark

ISBN 1-57035-662-9

Printed in China

Published and Distributed by

SOPRIS
WEST
EDUCATIONAL SERVICES

4093 Specialty Place • Longmont, CO 80504 • (303) 651-2829
www.sopriswest.com

How Does Your Garden Grow?

Book 7

UNITS 19 • 20 • 21

Read Well

Sopris West Educational Services

Theme

How Does Your Garden Grow?

Honeybee facts, a wild west fiction with Billy Bee, the story of a little rabbit with a green thumb, and Mother Goose team up to create a charming collection of springtime stories.

The Honeybee and the Robber

a moving/picture book by Eric Carle

Related Literature

THE CARROT SEED

Story by Ruth Krauss
Pictures by Crockett Johnson

Related Literature

SAM MCBRATNEY
Just You and Me
illustrated by IVAN BATES

Related Literature

Bees Buzzing

STORY I INTRODUCTION

Bees are very interesting.

Raise your hand if you've ever seen a bee.

Let's make a list of things we think we know about bees.

I think bees live in a hive, so I'm going to write that on the board.

What do you think you know about bees?
Write student responses.

Today we're going to read a story that tells facts about bees.

The title of the story is *Bee Facts*.
Everyone, what is the title? (*Bee Facts*)

Marilyn Sprick is the author.
Who wrote the story? (Marilyn Sprick)

The illustrator is Philip Weber.

Bee Facts

by Marilyn Sprick

Illustrated by Philip A. Weber, Jr.

Did you know that bees are insects?

Count the body parts. One, two, three.

Bees have a head, a thorax, and an abdomen.

Head

Thorax

Abdomen

One, two, three … three body parts!

Did you know that bees have six legs?

Count the legs. One, two, three, four, five, six.

Bees have six legs.

We just learned that bees are . . . (insects). That's one fact.

So, that means they have three . . . (body parts) and six . . . (legs).
That's two more . . . (facts).

Did you know that many bees live together in a hive?
The bees in the hive have different jobs.

Some are
worker bees.

Worker bees take care of many things in the hive.
They clean the honeycomb cells and feed the babies.

Some worker bees produce wax to make the
honeycomb cells.

What are some things the worker bees do?
(Clean the honeycomb cells, feed baby bees, make wax for the honeycomb cells)

Worker bees also guard the hive,
and they collect nectar from flowers.

Did you know that bees can talk to each other?

Bees can talk to each other. That's a . . . (fact).
How do you think bees talk to each other?

One of the ways bees talk to each other is by waggling their bodies.
This is called the waggle dance.

Everybody, let's waggle our bodies.

Bees use the waggle dance
to tell each other about food.

The waggle dance tells other bees how far away the food is.

The waggle dance tells other bees what direction the food is in.

The waggle dance even tells the other bees how high the food is.

Another way bees talk to each other is by buzzing while they dance. Did you know that bees buzz in patterns?

Bzz, bzz, bzz, bzz means
that the food is close by.

(Everybody, let's do four short buzzes to show that the food is close by.)

Bzz, bzz, bzz, bzzzzzzzzz, bzzzzzzzzz
means the food is far away.

(Everybody, let's do five buzzes to show that the food is far away.)

We sure learned a lot about bees.
Do you think bees are interesting insects?

PROCEED TO FACT SUMMARY

Fact Summary

Let's review what we learned about bees.

One, bees are insects.
>   That means that bees have three . . . (body parts)
>   and six . . . (legs).

Two, lots of bees live together in a . . . (hive).

Three, worker bees do many things to help take care of the hive. They . . .
>   (clean the honeycomb)
>   (feed the babies)
>   (produce wax to make the honeycomb)
>   (guard the hive)
>   (collect the nectar)

Four, bees can talk to . . . (each other).

Raise your hand if you remember any other facts about bees. (They use the waggle dance and buzzing to talk to each other. They talk to each other about food. They tell each other what direction the food is, how far away the food is, and how high the food is.)

END OF STORY 1

TIP

This story incorporates a song that is on
the *Read Well* CD—"Wiggle Waggle Dance."
You may wish to use the CD at that point in the story.

STORY 2 INTRODUCTION

Last time, we learned that bees are insects.

So, how many body parts does a bee have? (Three)

And how many legs? (Six)

We learned that bees live together in a hive and that
worker bees do many different things in the hive.

We also learned that bees talk to each other about food by . . .
(waggling their bodies), and by . . . (buzzing).

Today we're going to read a fun story about a worker bee.
This story is called *Billy Bee Out West.*

Richard Dunn *and* Shelley V. Jones *wrote the story. They are the* . . . (authors).

Philip Weber *drew the pictures. He is the* . . . (illustrator).

Billy Bee Out West

by Richard Dunn and Shelley V. Jones
Song lyrics by Shelley V. Jones and Richard Dunn
Illustrated by Philip A. Weber, Jr.

Billy Bee was a worker bee from the Okay Hive.
He spent all his days wandering far and wide, gathering nectar.

One day Billy twitched his antennae
and got a whiff of the most delicious smell.

Who is the story about? (A worker bee named Billy Bee)

At the beginning of the story, Billy Bee got a whiff of a most
delicious . . . (smell).

What do you think it was that Billy Bee smelled?

14

Billy Bee pulled on his boots, grabbed his hat, and headed out of the hive. "Hee haw!" hollered Billy as he flew off toward the desert.

Everybody, say "Hee haw."

Billy flew and flew, but all he saw was the dry desert floor. Just as Billy was growing tired, his antennae twitched and he smelled the most delicious smell.

There in the middle of the vast desert sands was a lone saguaro cactus with a flower in bloom.

What Billy Bee had smelled was a saguaro cactus . . . (flower).

Billy stopped in his tracks. He threw down his hat and yelled,
"Hee haw!" All his life Billy had heard the old geezers tell stories
of the great saguaro cactus flower. Legend had it that the flower
bloomed for only one night and was gone by high noon the next day.

What do you think Billy Bee is going to do?

"Hee haw!" shouted Billy. "I've got to go tell the others."

How do you think Billy is going to tell the other bees about the cactus flower?
(By doing the waggle dance and buzzing)

Billy made a beeline
towards his hive.
As Billy approached
the hive, he gave one
more, "Hee haw!"

Then Billy began
to buzz and do the
waggle dance.

Waggle Dance

Flap your wings to the
wiggle waggle dance.

Wiggle your bottom for the
wiggle waggle dance.

Stomp your feet for the
wiggle waggle dance.

Clap your hands for the
wiggle waggle dance.

Where is the honey?
Where can it be?

Sitting in a flower?
Hiding in a tree?

Don't you worry.
I'll show you.

With the wiggle waggle dance,
you'll know too.

In the middle of the story, Billy found the most
delicious smell. It was a saguaro cactus . . . (flower).

Billy flew back to the hive and told the other bees
by doing the . . . (waggle dance) and . . . (buzzing).

One by one the other bees followed Billy's directions to the saguaro cactus and its sweet golden nectar. The bees all buzzed in great excitement. "Hee haw for Billy!" shouted the bees.

Let's all "Hee haw" for Billy.

Before high noon, the bees had collected the nectar
and were on their way back to their hive.

After the bees followed Billy's directions to the cactus, they collected the . . . (nectar).
Then they went back to their . . . (hive).

Legend has it that
Billy Bee found three
saguaro cactus flowers
in his lifetime. Billy Bee
is a hero in the Bee Hall
of Fame.

PROCEED TO STORY SUMMARY

Story Summary

Let's retell our story.

Who is the story about? (A worker bee named Billy Bee)

 What happened at the beginning of the story? (Billy Bee got a whiff of a most delicious smell.)

Everyone, look at the picture. It will help you remember the middle part of the story. What happened in the middle of the story? (Billy found the most delicious smell. It was a saguaro cactus flower. Billy flew back to the hive and told the other bees.)

What happened at the end of the story?
(The bees in the hive followed Billy's directions to the cactus;
they collected the nectar; they took the nectar back to the hive.)

READER RESPONSE:

Billy Bee ended up being a hero in the Bee Hall of Fame.
Have you ever found or done something for others and felt like a hero?

END OF STORY 2

See Teacher's Guide for related activities—Pocket Chart Retell and Bookmaking.

Flowers Growing

STORY 1 INTRODUCTION

Flowers are very interesting.

Raise your hand if you like flowers.

Let's make a list of things we *think*
we know about flowers.

I think flowers grow in the ground,
so I'm going to write that down.

What do you think you know about flowers?

Write student responses.

Our story today tells facts about flowers.

The title of the story is *Flower Facts*.
Everyone, what is the title? (*Flower Facts*)

Richard Dunn and Shelley V. Jones wrote the story.
They are the . . . (authors).

The person who drew the pictures is Larry Nolte.
Who is the illustrator? (Larry Nolte)

Flower Facts

by Richard Dunn and Shelley V. Jones

Illustrated by Larry Nolte

Did you know that all flowers start off as a seed?

Flower seeds come in all colors, shapes, and sizes. Some seeds fall to the ground near the flower that made them. Some seeds are blown by the wind. Other seeds are scattered by birds and animals. Still other seeds are planted by people.

All flowers start as a . . . (seed). That is a fact.

How are seeds spread around? (Some fall to the ground, some blow in the wind, some are scattered by animals, and some are planted.)

Did you know that most seeds need good soil to grow into a healthy flower? When a seed first begins to grow, roots dig down into the soil. The roots gather water and food from the soil. The roots hold the plant in place.

What do the roots do? (Gather water and food; hold the plant in place)

Did you know that the stem and leaves push their way through the soil? The stem and leaves try to find the sunlight. The sunlight gives the plant energy so flowers can grow.

What do the stem and leaves grow towards? (The sun)

The energy of the sun helps flowers . . . (grow).

Did you know that flowers need three things to grow?

One…
flowers need water.

Two…
flowers need sunlight.

Three…
flowers need air.

Let's name three things a flower needs to grow.
One . . . (water), two . . . (sunlight), and three . . . (air).

Did you know that once a flower grows,
it will make brand new seeds?

What do you think will happen to those seeds?

PROCEED TO FACT SUMMARY

Fact Summary

Let's review what we learned about flowers in this story.

All flowers start off as . . . (seeds).

When a flower first starts to grow,
its roots dig down into the . . . (soil).

The roots gather water and . . . (food)
from the soil.

Flowers need three things to grow.
They are . . . (water, sunlight, and air).

Raise your hand if you remember other things we
learned about flowers. (Flower seeds come in all shapes
and sizes; a flower's roots hold it in place in the ground;
a flower's stem and leaves push through the soil to find
sunlight; sunlight gives the plant energy so the flower
can grow.)

END OF STORY 1

STORY 2 INTRODUCTION

Last time, we learned some facts about flowers.

What do all flowers start off as? (Seeds)

What are three things a flower needs to grow?
(Water, sunlight, air)

The title of today's story is *Felicia's Flower*.

Look at the picture.
What do you think Felicia is? (A rabbit)

Shelley V. Jones is the author of the story.
Who wrote the story? (Shelley V. Jones)

Larry Nolte drew the pictures for the story.
He is the . . . (illustrator).

Felicia's Flower

by Shelley V. Jones
Illustrated by Larry Nolte

Felicia loved beautiful things. Her rabbit hole was full of the beautiful things that she had collected. Of all the things Felicia had, her flower garden was her pride and joy. All the rabbits in the neighborhood admired the many colors of her garden.

What colors do you see in Felicia's garden?

36

Felicia's neighbors often said, "Felicia, what lovely flowers!"
This made Felicia happy. She would puff up with pride and say,
"Yes, they are beautiful, aren't they?"

Show me how Felicia looked when her neighbors complimented her garden.

Felicia's neighbors often asked, "Felicia, what makes your garden
so beautiful?" But Felicia just said, "Oh, I have a green thumb."
Then Felicia would disappear into her rabbit hole—without sharing her secret.

Did Felicia tell her neighbors how to make a beautiful garden?
She kept it a secret, didn't she?

Felicia said she had a green thumb, but Felicia knew that her flowers needed three things.

Name three things that flowers need. (Water, sunlight, and air)

So, what do you think Felicia did?

She watered her flowers every day.

She pulled the weeds so her flowers could get air and sunlight.

Day after day Felicia worked alone in the quiet of her garden. When someone asked, "Felicia, what makes your garden so beautiful?" Felicia would just say, "Oh, I have a green thumb." Then she would disappear into her rabbit hole—without sharing her secret.

At the beginning of the story, Felicia had a beautiful . . . (garden).
But when her neighbors asked how she made her garden beautiful,
she wouldn't share her . . . (secret).

One day when Felicia went outside, she noticed
something in the corner of her garden.
She hopped closer to take a look.

What do you think Felicia saw?

It was the biggest seed Felicia had ever seen!
Felicia clapped her hands with delight.

Clap your hands like Felicia.
How do you think she felt?
What do you think Felicia
should do with the seed?

Felicia got out her gardening tools and planted the huge seed.

Day after day Felicia watered the seed and pulled the weeds around it. Day after day nothing sprouted, nothing grew. Felicia said, "Surely the seed should have sprouted by now." Then Felicia sighed, but she didn't give up.

This is how to sigh.

Everyone, sigh.

How do you think Felicia felt?

She didn't give up. Everyday, she . . . (watered the seed), and she pulled the . . . (weeds) around it.

One day Felicia woke up and couldn't
see out of her rabbit hole. "Goodness gracious!
What is blocking my front door?" she thought. She climbed
out through the back of her rabbit hole, and then stared up
in amazement. Towering above her was a big, green pole.

What do you think the green pole was?

One by one, Felicia's neighbors gathered and stared at the huge green pole. "I think you should chop it down," said one neighbor.

"I think you should climb up to the top to see what it is!" said another neighbor. Felicia began doing just that.

Raise your hand if you think she should chop down the big green pole.
Raise your hand if you think she should climb to the top and see what it is.

44

Felicia climbed higher and higher. Just when she thought she couldn't possibly climb any higher, she spotted a huge flower. "Goodness gracious!" said Felicia.

"Why, it's a flower!" exclaimed Felicia. "It looks just like the sun. I'm going to call it a sunflower."

Why did Felicia decide to call the flower a sunflower? (It looked like the sun.)

Felicia climbed onto the big flower and looked down.
She waved and her good neighbors cheered.

"It's a sunflower!" Felicia shouted.

Felicia sat on the sunflower enjoying the sun. Just as
Felicia began to wonder how she was going to get down,
the stem began to bend. Slowly Felicia was lowered to
the ground.

Pretend your hand is the sunflower and your arm is the stem.
Show me how Felicia was lowered to the ground.

As Felicia jumped from the flower, she and her neighbors were showered with seeds from the sunflower. "Oo! Aah!" chorused the crowd. "Thank you, Felicia. Thank you for the seeds."

Felicia was a little surprised. She hadn't planned on sharing the sunflower seeds. But she shrugged and said, 'You're welcome." Then Felicia helped her neighbors plant the seeds here, there, and everywhere—all around the neighborhood.

Do you think Felicia enjoyed helping her neighbors?

Now when visitors come, Felicia and her neighbors often hear, "Oh, what a beautiful neighborhood! What beautiful flowers!" Felicia always asks, "Would you like some seeds? We'd love to tell you the secret for growing beautiful flowers."

Who can name the three things flowers need to grow? (Water, sunlight and air)

48

PROCEED TO STORY SUMMARY

Story Summary

Let's retell our story.

Who is the story about? (A rabbit named Felicia)

● What happened at the beginning of the story?
(Felicia had a beautiful garden; she wouldn't tell her neighbors how she made her garden beautiful.)

■ Everyone, look at the picture. It will help you remember the middle part of the story. What happened in the middle of the story? (Felicia found a big seed; she planted the seed, and then she watered it and weeded around it. The seed grew into a big, tall plant.)

▲ What happened at the end of the story?
(Felicia climbed up the plant; as she was lowered
to the ground, seeds fell from the sunflower.
Felicia helped her neighbors plant and take care
of the seeds. They all had beautiful gardens.)

READER RESPONSE:

At the end of the story when Felicia helped her neighbors, she felt happy.

How do you feel when you help people?

END OF STORY 2

See Teacher's Guide for related activities—Pocket Chart Retell and Bookmaking.

Mother Goose

Story 1 • Meet Mother Goose

Story 2 • Goose, Goose, Goose, Goose, Duck

STORY 1 INTRODUCTION

The title of this story is *Meet Mother Goose*.

Everyone, what is the title? (*Meet Mother Goose*)

The author of the story is Mrs. B.

The illustrator of the story is Susan Jerde.
Who drew the pictures? (Susan Jerde)

This story is about Mother Goose nursery rhymes.

Meet Mother Goose

by Mrs. B

Illustrated by Susan Jerde

Mother Goose nursery rhymes and poems have been told for many, many years. No one is really quite sure who wrote them.

Children all around the world enjoy Mother Goose. You may have heard some of these rhymes and poems before.

I'm going to read some Mother Goose nursery rhymes. If you know them, join in with me as I read.

56

It's Raining, It's Pouring

It's raining,
it's pouring,

The old man is snoring.

He bumped his head
when he went to bed,

And he couldn't get up
in the morning.

Little Miss Muffet

Little Miss Muffet
Sat on a tuffet,
Eating her curds and whey.
Along came a spider
Who sat down beside her
And frightened
Miss Muffet away.

Jack and Jill

Jack and Jill
went up the hill,

To fetch a
pail of water.

Jack fell down
and broke his crown,

And Jill came
tumbling after.

Many nursery rhymes have words that rhyme. Listen for the rhyming words in "One, Two, Buckle My Shoe."

One, Two,
Buckle My Shoe

One, two,
Buckle my shoe.

Three, four,
Shut the door.

Five, six,
Pick up sticks.

Seven, eight,
Lay them straight.

Nine, ten,
A big, fat hen.

I'm going to say the rhyme again, only this time I'm going to leave out some words.
You can tell me the word that is missing in each line.

One, two, buckle my . . . (shoe). Three, four, shut the . . . (door).
Five, six, pick up . . . (sticks). Seven, eight, lay them . . . (straight).
Nine, ten, a big fat . . . (hen).

Listen for the rhyming words in "Humpty Dumpty."

Humpty Dumpty

Humpty Dumpty sat on a wall.
Humpty Dumpty had a great fall.

All the king's horses and
all the king's men,

Couldn't put Humpty
together again.

I'm going to say this rhyme again, and I want you to fill in the words I leave out.

Humpty Dumpty sat on a wall.
Humpty Dumpty had a great . . . (fall).
All the king's horses and all the king's men,
Couldn't put Humpty together . . . (again).

Let's have fun with one more Mother Goose nursery rhyme.

Pat-a-Cake

Pat-a-cake,
pat-a-cake,

Baker's man.
Bake me a cake
As fast as you can.
Pat it and prick it,

And mark it
with G.

Put it in the oven
For you and me.

We can really have fun by changing some of the words in that rhyme. Listen …

Pat-a-cake, pat-a-cake,
Baker's man.
Bake me a cake
As fast as you f-f-f fan.

Pat-a-cake, pat-a-cake,
Baker's man.
Bake me a cake
As fast as you p-p-p pan.

Pat-a-cake, pat-a-cake,
Baker's man.
Bake me a cake
As fast as you r-r-r ran.

Pat-a-cake, pat-a-cake,
Baker's man.
Bake me a cake
As fast as you m-m-m man.

END OF STORY I

63

STORY 2 INTRODUCTION

Last time we read about Mother Goose's nursery rhymes.

Today's story is a made-up story about another Mother Goose, and her five little babies.

This story is called *Goose, Goose, Goose, Goose, Duck.*
Everyone, what is the title? (*Goose, Goose, Goose, Goose, Duck*)

The story is by Marilyn Sprick.
Who is the author of the story? (Marilyn Sprick)

The person who drew the pictures is Susan Jerde.

Goose, Goose, Goose, Goose, Duck

by Marilyn Sprick

Illustrated by Susan Jerde

For 28 days, Mother Goose had been sitting patiently on her eggs.

Every morning, she would get off her nest and count her eggs.
One, two, three, four, five.

Five beautiful eggs!

There were four great big eggs and one small egg . . .
and Mother Goose loved them all.

Mother Goose had four eggs that were . . . (big) and one egg that was . . . (small).

Early one morning, Mother Goose heard a "scratch, scratch, scratch" coming from her eggs. Before long, two fine little baby geese hatched from two of the big eggs.

Mother Goose called the first little goose, Bruce, and the second little goose, Moose.

Everyone, what did Mother Goose call the first two baby geese? (Bruce and Moose)

As the sun rose, Bruce and Moose heard "PLOP, plop, plop" and "snort, snort, snort."

Moose said with alarm, "What is that?"

Bruce said, "Oh no! I think the sky is falling!"

Everyone, what did Bruce Goose say? (Oh no! I think the sky is falling!)

Mother Goose said to her children, "Do not be alarmed."

Then she sang a little song, "It's raining. It's pouring. The old man is snoring. He bumped his head when he went to bed, and he couldn't get up in the morning."

Everyone, sing the song with me. (It's raining . . .)

"Honk! Honk!" cheered the two little geese. They were no longer worried.

Why do you think the two little geese were no longer worried?

Soon Mother Goose heard another "scratch, scratch, scratch" coming from her eggs.

Another big egg cracked open, and out popped another little goose.

Mother Goose sang happily, "One little, two little, three little geese..."

Everyone, sing Mother Goose's counting song. (One little, two little...)

Mother Goose called the third little goose, Juice.

Mother Goose has three little geese—Bruce, Moose, and... (Juice).

70

Just as the clock struck one, the three little geese—Bruce, Moose, and Juice— heard a terrific clatter. They didn't know what to do.

Juice asked her mother, "What's the matter?"

Moose honked, "What's that clatter?"

And Bruce said, "Oh no! I think the sky is falling!"

Everyone, what did Bruce Goose say? (Oh no! I think the sky is falling!)

Mother Goose said, "You silly little geese. Jack and Jill went up the hill to fetch a pail of water. Jack fell down and broke his crown, and Jill came tumbling after."

Everyone, help me say what Mother Goose told her little geese. (Jack and Jill went up the hill to fetch a pail of water. Jack fell down and broke his crown, and Jill came tumbling after.)

"Honk," said Moose.

"Honk, honk," said Bruce.

And Juice said, "That's so sad." Then the three little geese began to cry.

Mother Goose said, "Silly little geese. Jack fixed his crown, and Jill is fine."

As the sun was setting, Mother Goose heard "scratch, scratch, scratch" coming from the eggs again.

The last big egg cracked, and one more little goose hatched.

Mother Goose sang, "One little, two little, three little geese, four little geese in all."

Everyone, sing Mother Goose's counting song. (One little, two little . . .)

Mother Goose named the fourth little goose, Caboose.

Now Mother Goose has four little geese—Bruce, Moose, Juice, and . . . (Caboose).

The sky was turning dark when Mother Goose and Bruce, Moose, Juice, and Caboose heard a *very* strange noise the—strangest noise of all.

"Honk, honk, honk, honk," chorused the four little geese.

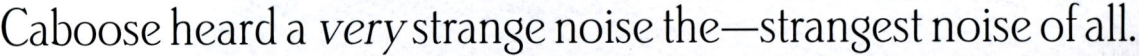

Caboose squawked, "What's that?"

Moose honked, "Is it a cat?"

Juice said, "It can't be a rat!"

And Bruce said, "Oh no! I think the sky is falling!"

Even Mother Goose was worried.
She said, "I don't know what that strange noise is."

Mother Goose counted her little geese. "One little, two little, three little geese, four little geese in all."

Then Mother Goose stood up to check on her last egg—the little egg.

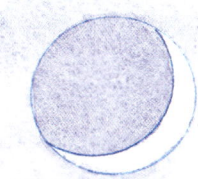

All she found were pieces of the shell.
What do you think happened to the last little egg?

Just then, the geese heard the very strange noise again.
The four little geese began to honk, so Mother Goose said,
"Hush little babies, don't say a word."

When her babies quieted down, Mother Goose listened carefully. From the pond, she could hear the croaking of frogs … and the very strange noise.
What do you think is making the strange noise?

In the light of the moon, Mother Goose could see the small shadow of her fifth little goose paddling near the shore.

"Quack, quack, quack," cried the fifth little goose. "Where is my mother?"

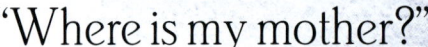

Mother Goose waddled to the shore, and cuddled the fifth little goose close to her. She said, "Roses are red. Violets are blue. Sugar is sweet. And so are you."

"Quack!" said the little bird.

"What a strange little goose you are," said Mother Goose. "But I love you just the same."

And Mother Goose named her littlest goose, Duck.

Why do you think Mother Goose named her littlest goose, Duck?

It had been a long day, so Mother Goose put her babies to bed.

As Mother Goose settled down for a rest, she thought of taking her babies to town.

What fun it would be! They would waddle proudly in a row to meet Wee Willie Winkie, Old Mother Hubbard, and all the rest of her dear friends.

Honk! Honk! Honk! Honk! Quack!

Tell me what the little geese said.

Honk! Honk! Honk! Honk! Quack!

What do you think Wee Willie Winkie and Old Mother Hubbard will think when they see Mother Goose and her babies?

PROCEED TO STORY SUMMARY

Story Summary

Let's retell our story.

Who is the story about? (Mother Goose and her babies)

What happened at the beginning of the story?

Mother Goose had five beautiful . . . (eggs).
She had four eggs that were . . . (big) and
one egg that was . . . (small).

Everyone, look at the picture. It will
help you remember the middle part
of the story. What happened in the
middle of the story?

The eggs cracked open and out
popped the little . . . (geese).

The little geese heard a strange . . .
(noise).

What happened at the end of the story?

The last egg cracked open and the fifth little bird said . . . (quack).

What was the last little bird? (A duck)

READER RESPONSE:

I liked this story because Mother Goose loved the little duck even though he was different.

What did you like about the story?

END OF STORY 2

See Teacher's Guide for related activities—Pocket Chart Retell and Bookmaking.

Mrs. B is a teacher at the Ant School in the *Read Well K* stories. She is featured throughout the program, and is also the acronym for the author of many of the stories in *Read Well K*. When program authors found that shared story writing allowed them to combine their talents, Mrs. B was the designated author. Mrs. B stands for Marilyn, Richard, Shelley, and Barbara.

M is for Marilyn Sprick.

Marilyn Maeda Sprick is a third generation Japanese American. She and her husband, Randy, have two grown children. They live in the woods near Eugene, Oregon, with their two dogs. Marilyn has always loved writing and art, but most of all she loves teaching children of all ages how to read well.

R is for Richard Dunn.

Richard Dunn is a kindergarten teacher in Seattle, Washington. He lives with his wife, two children, and a big white cat. During his free time, Richard loves to play with his children, read, and spend time outdoors hiking and camping.

S is for Shelley V. Jones.

Shelley V. Jones teaches in Oregon and lives with her husband and a beagle named Macintosh. She is a mom with two grown kids. Shelley loves books and music, and has spent her life teaching reading and music to people of all ages.

B is for Barbara Gunn.

Barbara Gunn grew up in California, where she spent her summers swimming, bike riding, and making up stories. Now she lives in Eugene, Oregon, with her husband, Steve, and two cats, Oreo and Tillie. Barbara has two grown children. She still likes making up stories, and especially enjoys researching how to teach children to read well.

Philip A. Weber, Jr. was born and raised in Dallas, Texas. Philip began drawing as soon as he could hold a pencil. He has lots of interests including cooking, drawing, and collecting comic books. He is also a character voice actor and loves puppetry and skiing. He now lives in Michigan with his wife, Linda, two little girls—Brooke and Madison, and their cat Maddie.

Larry Nolte doodles for a living. He has published a number of children's books, which together are taller than a stack of pancakes. He lives on the south side of St. Louis in an old "arts and crafts" style house with his lovely wife, three wonderful children and a most unique dog.

Susan Jerde lives in Eugene, Oregon with her husband, a dog, two cats, and two fishponds. She has a daughter away at college. She has loved to draw since she was a little girl, especially animals. When she isn't drawing pictures she likes to ride horses and go camping with her family. Susan also grows lots of fruits, vegetables and flowers in her garden.